THE ONE-LEGGED GURU

A ONE-ACT PLAY

ANDREW BISS

Original cover images © Toniflap

Cover design by Ernest Waggenheim

First Printing, 2017

ISBN-13: 978-1547247752
ISBN-10: 1547247754

ENTR'ACTE
EDITIONS

"And now here is my secret, a very simple secret: it is only with the heart that one can see rightly; what is essential is invisible to the eye."

— Antoine de Saint-Exupéry

CHARACTERS

JACK: Plain-spoken and pragmatic with a somewhat caustic edge. A personality discoloured by cynicism. 20s/50s.

RACHEL: Jack's wife. Well-disposed despite her circumstances. Unassuming with an independent streak. Appealing. 20s/50s.

SETTING & TIME

SETTING: The living room of Jack and Rachel's London flat.

TIME: Night. The present.

The One-Eyed Guru was first performed at Youngstown State University's College of Fine and Performing Arts in Youngstown, Ohio in 2005.

THE ONE-EYED GURU

At Rise: In a dimly lit living room JACK is found seated on a sofa, head in hands, a phone on the coffee table in front of him. After a while the phone begins to ring. He answers it immediately.

JACK: Hello? (*Beat.*) No, I don't. I just told you I didn't!

> (*JACK hangs up the phone abruptly. Momentarily there is heard the sound of a door opening and closing offstage.*)

RACHEL: (*Off.*) Jack? Jack, are you up?

> (*RACHEL enters, somewhat distraught.*)

RACHEL: Jack...Jack? (*She switches on an additional light. With a sigh of relief.*) Oh, thank God, there you are!

JACK: (*Angrily.*) I think that's my line, actually? Where the fuck have you been, for God's sake?

RACHEL: Oh, Jack, oh God, I'm so sorry. Oh, don't be cross, please don't, please! I meant to call you. I tried, I did honestly, but–

JACK: Do you know what time it is? Do you have any idea what I've–

RACHEL: I know, I know–

JACK: No you don't know! You don't have a clue. I've been worried sick. I've called the police, the hospitals, your parents, the–

3

RACHEL: Oh, shit! Shit! I know, I know. I know you think that I don't, but I do. I know I should've phoned, but I couldn't. I couldn't, Jack, believe me.

JACK: Couldn't – or couldn't be bothered?

RACHEL: *Couldn't*, Jack, I couldn't. (*Beat.*) Sometimes… sometimes things just happen, completely unexpected things. Things that…that you have no control over and…and that's what happened to me…tonight…today. I thought of you, of course. I thought of you often. But I couldn't call you. I was…I was somewhere else.

JACK: You don't say? (*Beat.*) Phew, well that's that taken care of. Good, good I feel much better now. Thank you for that.

RACHEL: (*Insistent.*) Jack, listen to me, I couldn't.

JACK: Why, because you forgot the number? Or were your fingers temporarily paralyzed?

RACHEL: Of course not, I just…

JACK: Just what? You just didn't think is what you just. You just didn't stop for one minute to think about me – about the worry you'd cause, about what I might be thinking. God, if you knew…if you'd seen some of the scenarios I'd had going through my head… (*Shaking his head.*) I don't even want to think about it now.

RACHEL: (*A deep sigh, then methodically.*) Look, I know it was wrong. I know I should've called and I didn't. I didn't mean to make you worry. It was irresponsible and I apologise – I do really. But I can't change what's already happened. And I'm here

4

now and I'm all right – I'm fine, as you can see. Actually, I…I'm more than fine. (*With a self-conscious laugh.*) Actually, I…I feel great, actually.

JACK: (*Sarcastically.*) Do you, actually? Oh, that's fantastic!

RACHEL: Oh, Jack, don't be like that, please. If you'll just let me explain you'll understand everything.

JACK: Yes, of course I will.

RACHEL: (*Insistent.*) Yes you will – I promise you will. It'll all be clear, everything will make sense – just like it did for me. Just hear me out…please.

JACK: Oh, I'll hear you out. You needn't think I'm going to sit up half the night waiting for you without expecting to hear a bloody good explanation as to why.

RACHEL: Only, try to be open-minded about what I'm about to tell you, because…well, just try to keep an open mind, that's all.

JACK: (*Coldly.*) I said I'd listen, and that's what I'll do.

RACHEL: Okay, all right, all right. (*Beat.*) I…well, it all began at the top of King Street at about three-thirty this afternoon and I…God, that sounds like I just made it up, doesn't it?

JACK: Did you?

RACHEL: (*Beat.*) Do you want to hear this or don't you?

JACK: I said I'd listen, and I'm listening.

RACHEL: Okay. So I… (*Standing and moving upstage R. to the drinks cabinet.*) Look, if you don't mind I'm going to pour myself a quick nightcap – I think I need a stiffener.

JACK: Another one?

RACHEL: What?

JACK: Never mind.

RACHEL: I thought you said, "Another one?"

JACK: I thought you said, "What?"

RACHEL: (*Beat.*) Do you want one?

JACK: No.

RACHEL: (*As she pours her drink.*) So…anyway, I'd just stepped outside of Marks & Spencer's and was pointing myself toward the bus stop, feeling more than a little bit pissed off to tell you the truth, because they'd had a taupe jacket in there that I'd–

JACK: A what?

RACHEL: A taupe jacket.

JACK: What in God's name is taupe?

RACHEL: It's a colour.

JACK: (*After a sigh.*) All right, carry on.

RACHEL: (*Returning with her drink.*) Anyway, I'd had my eye on it for quite some time, and I'd tried it on more than once to see if I thought it suited me or not. So, after yet another mental tug-of-war over need versus want, and feeling guilty about people in Somalia with no arms, I'd finally plucked up the courage to go in and buy it, only to be informed that after all that they didn't even have my size in stock anymore. So off I strode, marching down the street with a severe case of the-world-hates-my-guts-and-the-feeling's-mutual, and just an over all sense of being persecuted and conspired against in general, when suddenly this old man threw himself in front of me – I mean literally threw himself – and almost sent me flying! Of course my knee-jerk English reaction was to apologise as graciously as possible and hurry way in embarrassment. But for some unknown reason some semblance of clarity rose to the surface, and I realised that it wasn't my fault and I shouldn't apologise, and so I didn't; I just glared at him and waited for him to. But he didn't either: he simply stared at me. So I said, "Don't look at me like that, it was your fault." But still he said nothing – just stared. So I sort of sneered at him as best I could and said, "I see – too important to say you're sorry, I suppose?" But he just smiled at me. Not a mean-spirited smile – more kindly than anything. And all he said was, "What's wrong?"

(*Pause.*)

JACK: And you said, "You."

RACHEL: No, I didn't, I…I couldn't somehow. There was something about…his face, the way he was looking at me…I didn't know what to say.

JACK: And then, like an idiot, you apologised.

RACHEL: No, I didn't. I told you I didn't. And actually, the longer I stood there the more angry I became – really angry, actually – and I was half tempted to say, "Look, you blind old bastard, why the hell don't you watch where you're walking!" But I didn't. I controlled myself and calmed myself, and…I don't know…it was the way his eyes were looking at me – into me. It sounds ridiculous, but it was as though I felt compelled to tell him the truth.

JACK: About him being a blind old bastard?

RACHEL: (*A little impatient.*) Of course not. About why I was upset.

JACK: And did you?

RACHEL: Well how could I? What was I going to do, relate to him the heartbreaking tragedy of my obsession with a taupe-coloured jacket in Marks & Spencer's over several weeks of my precious and very limited life span, and how I'd just now discovered that they'd viciously and quite vindictively neglected to stock up on the very size that would have temporarily filled a vacuum in my pathetic consumer-driven existence? (*Beat.*) I told him the only thing I could tell him.

JACK: Which was?

RACHEL: I said, "Nothing's wrong." And then I burst into tears.

JACK: You did what?

RACHEL: I started crying – I couldn't help it.

JACK: Over the jacket?

RACHEL: (*With irritation.*) No, not over the jacket.

JACK: Well what then? Are you depressed?

RACHEL: No…not as far as I know. I just…He was just…

(*Pause.*)

JACK: Oh, well thank you. Thank you for allaying my fears; that explains everything. I'm glad you've been able put my mind at rest. Now, if you wouldn't mind just skimming over what happened in the intervening eight hours between then and now, I'd say we could safely describe this evening as having been a resounding success, don't you?

RACHEL: (*With a smile.*) Oh, poor Jack, I must sound completely bonkers right now, mustn't I? This must all sound so peculiar. But if you'd been there, if you'd…*felt* the way he looked at you – the way he looked at me – you'd have understood. I know you would.

JACK: So you keep saying.

RACHEL: And when he took my hand, I–

JACK: He did what?

RACHEL: Took my hand. He reached out and took my hand and held it in his, and…and when he did, I–

JACK: (*Incredulous.*) You mean to say, you let a complete stranger – a man – start mauling you in the middle of King Street?

RACHEL: He didn't maul me. I told you, he held my hand. He

was an old man, for God's sake, and I was...I was upset, I was crying, I...It was natural.

JACK: Yeah, well we'll get back to that part later...and we will.

RACHEL: The point is, when he did touch me – when his skin touched my skin – I felt...I felt this incredible sensation all over me, over my entire body. It was like a shock, almost like an electrical shock. But not uncomfortable, just...hard to describe, really, just...odd.

JACK: I believe in medical circles it's often referred to as the female orgasm.

RACHEL: (*With frustration.*) I'm trying to tell you something, Jack.

JACK: So was he, by the sounds of it.

RACHEL: All right, if you're going to go on like that, then... then don't bother. Just go. Just...go to bed! (*Beat.*) For Christ's sake, I'm trying to explain something that happened to me today; something big, something...and if all you can do is sit there and make snide, insinuating remarks then...then there's not much point, is there?

JACK: (*Beat.*) Okay, okay, I'm... I was being flippant... I'm sorry

RACHEL: I doubt very much that you are. But I think you would be if you knew the truth.

JACK: Which is?

RACHEL: I don't think you want to know?

JACK: (*Condescendingly.*) I want to know.

RACHEL: Very well then, I'll tell you. (*Beat.*) You see, when he took my hand – this stranger – he suddenly stopped being a stranger. He became familiar. I knew him. I didn't know from where or when, but I knew him. It was as if he were…I don't know, family, or…or an old friend I'd lost touch with. I know it sounds insane, and I…I can't really explain it – not even to myself – but I…I knew him.

JACK: Small world. So who was he?

RACHEL: I told you, I don't know.

JACK: Well, what was his name?

RACHEL: I don't know, I didn't ask him. It seems silly now, but–

JACK: Yes, it does seem silly.

RACHEL: I… It didn't seem important, somehow.

JACK: (*With a sigh.*) Look, I am trying to understand, Rachel – I am, really – but quite honestly, so far what you've told me is about nine tenths of nothing.

RACHEL: Because I'm still telling you – or trying to – that's why. Let me finish.

(*JACK raises his hands in appeasement. RACHEL takes a sip from her drink before continuing.*)

RACHEL: So…well then he asked me if he could buy me a cup

of tea – just so I could get myself together, and…and things…and so we did.

JACK: And?

RACHEL: And then we talked. And we talked. And talked, and talked and talked.

JACK: About?

RACHEL: Everything. Anything. It really didn't seem to matter *what* we talked about – we just talked. It was…well, you know what it's like when you meet up with an old friend.

JACK: An old friend?

RACHEL: Yes, a good friend that you haven't seen in donkey's years. Before you know it you're yakking away at each other nine to the dozen, and you start getting that weird feeling as though you'd just been speaking to each other the day before yesterday? Well that's how it was. It was exactly like that. I wish I could explain it better than I am, but–

JACK: But he wasn't – he's not an old friend.

RACHEL: I *know*, Jack – that's what I'm trying to tell you. Aren't you listening? The whole thing was so…*so completely bloody strange.*

JACK: And what did he do – for a living I mean? And I say, "did" on the assumption that he's as old as you say he is.

RACHEL: He's not retired – he's done the same thing all his life. He's a seer.

JACK: A seer?

RACHEL: Yes, a...a spiritual guide, a visionary. He sees things; he knows things, like a...a–

JACK: (*Impatiently.*) I know what a seer is.

RACHEL: Well you did ask.

JACK: (*Knowingly.*) I see. I get it now. My God, you really are a soft touch, aren't you? They must see you coming. You must give off some sort of scent. I mean, let's be honest, you've racked up some pretty idiotic credits on that dingbat resume of yours to date, but I'd say this just about warrants you a place in the half-wit hall of fame, wouldn't you?

RACHEL: (*With barely contained anger.*) Why do you do that? *This?* Does it make you feel bigger, cleverer than me, more masculine? Is that what it does for you when you start tossing around blame and insults, and put-downs, and...and making me feel like I don't know what the hell I'm doing with anything I'm doing at any time ever? (*Beat.*) For God's sake, you weren't even there!

JACK: More's the pity. That type's usually scared off by someone with half a brain. (*Beat.*) Asked you for money, did he?

RACHEL: (*Bluntly.*) No, he didn't.

JACK: That's news. So who pays his bills, the sacred spirits or the social security?

RACHEL: I don't know. I don't know how he makes his living. I assume normally he charges something, but quite honestly I really don't care. All I can tell you is that he didn't ask me for any money. And even if he had, I probably would've given it to him anyway. Not because I was under his spell, or to naïve or cretinous to know any better, but because he was kind. He was kind and I liked him.

JACK: Yeah, well I realised that when you told me you got weak at the knees the minute he touched you. And who paid for the tea?

RACHEL: I did.

JACK: (*Sarcastically.*) Really?

RACHEL: After a lot of squabbling and insisting.

JACK: Well yes, of course. So tell me, what sage old nuggets of insight did he dole out to you, this tea swilling witch doctor? Did he tell you that you'd experienced a time of great pain in your life, that someone in your family was ill, and that you had a natural affinity for the colour blue? Or was he more specific? Perhaps he revealed to you how the fates had deliberately kiboshed your attempts to buy that jacket in Marks & Spencer's in the certain knowledge that one day you'd discover another jacket in another chain store that was going to enrich your life beyond all human comprehension? Or perhaps he dug a little deeper and exposed to you the startling truth of your hidden inner core of complete and utter gullibility? Now, if he'd shown you that I really would be impressed.

RACHEL: (*Calmly.*) He told me he had a glass eye.

JACK: (*Laughing.*) He told you what?

RACHEL: (*Unmoved.*) That he had a glass eye.

JACK: A glass eye indeed…you don't say? Now that really is convincing. Very otherworldly. And how did he happen to come by it then, this glass eye: peered too deeply into some parallel universe, did he? Someone poked back, did they?

RACHEL: He lost it in a car accident when he was thirteen. His face went through the windscreen and a shard of glass became lodged in his eye. It was jagged – the glass – sort of like a fishhook. There was nothing they could do. The eyeball was removed with the glass still embedded.

JACK: (*Repulsed.*) For Christ's sake, you don't have to give me the details.

RACHEL: He said that afterwards, after he came out of the hospital – even after all the kindness and hard work from the doctors and nurses – the only thing that filled his thoughts was an overwhelming desire to kill himself. He couldn't feel anything – nothing but ugly and disfigured. Not just physically, but emotionally. He explained that after thirteen years of seeing his life from a dual perspective he could now view it only through a single aperture – like a camera – as if half of him had shut down. (*Beat.*) But he said that gradually, as time went on and he slowly began to find the strength to accept and adjust to his new reality, he began to be aware something quite peculiar. He found that, over time, although he'd lost the use of one of his eyes, he could now see twice as much as he could before.

(*Pause.*)

JACK: (*Nodding his head.*) Nice…very nice…nice hook. No pun intended.

RACHEL: Then he asked me to point to which of his eyes I

thought was the glass one. I stared at them for ages – longer than I remember – but it was impossible to tell. They both so looked real. They both seemed so…full of life.

JACK: They probably were.

RACHEL: Eventually, out of desperation, I pointed haphazardly at his right eye, but all he said was, "You see, you've no idea, have you?"

JACK: He was right about that at least.

RACHEL: He never did tell me.

JACK: And that makes him special, does it – this glass eye? You were impressed by that were you?

RACHEL: Not really. Actually it's a lot more common than I thought. He told me there are many people all around us with glass eyes; it's just that we can't tell simply by looking at that them.

JACK: Oh yes, I've heard that. It's all the rage now, apparently.

RACHEL: He said that some people are born with a glass eye.

JACK: Yes, I think I read that too, somewhere.

RACHEL: It's there from birth. It's a part of their makeup. They appear, on the outside, to be like anyone else. But they have two sides to them, and the eyes become the manifestation of their duality. One half functions quite normally, capable of warmth and caring, able to view what it sees for what it is, for its worth and value. But its vision is often skewed by the other eye – the glass eye. That eye sees only what it wants, what it desires. He says it has no conscience, sees no consequence. It sees no other. It sees only that for which it hungers, and its determination to satisfy its hunger is tunnel-visioned, cold, and utterly ruthless.

JACK: What a complete load of bollocks. You mean to tell me you spent eight hours in some greasy spoon listening to that claptrap? You must need your head examined.

RACHEL: I never said we were there the whole time.

JACK: Where?

RACHEL: The café.

JACK: Where were you then?

RACHEL: His flat.

JACK: What?

RACHEL: For about half that time we were in his flat.

> (*Beat.*)

JACK: (*Astonished.*) I don't believe you! I don't bloody believe you! I don't believe you could be that stupid! I mean, I do, but–

RACHEL: There was nothing to worry about, Jack, I mean, come on, he–

JACK: Don't you...have you any idea...you know, sometimes I, I wonder if...sometimes I feel like I have no idea who you are. I mean...I mean, how could you be so bloody reckless, so irresponsible, so…*fucking stupid?*

RACHEL: Oh for God's sake, Jack, stop it. He was just an old man with a glass eye; what the hell was I supposed to be afraid of?

JACK: Old with a glass eye? Yes, of course, because that would stop him from doing…what, exactly? (*Insistent.*) Tell me – what?

RACHEL: (*Frustrated.*) Nothing, I suppose.

JACK: Hmm?

RACHEL: Nothing! (*Beat.*) But the point is, never – not at any time – did I ever feel like I was in any danger. I knew he wouldn't hurt me. I don't know how I knew, I just knew. (*Beat.*) And besides, he said there were things he needed to tell me; things he couldn't tell me in a public place because he didn't know how I might react. Important things, Jack. Things about my life – about me.

JACK: (*With a sigh.*) I give up with you sometimes, Rachel. Honestly, I just give up.

RACHEL: I never said I didn't have my guard up. I didn't say I wasn't nervous, or apprehensive, or, or…I was. Despite what my instincts told me, the fact was he was still a question mark. And as for what he wanted to tell me, well, God, you can imagine, can't you? My mind boggled and my heart skipped a beat.

JACK: (*Mockingly.*) Yes, of course.

RACHEL: Well, yours might not have, but mine did. But, still, there was always something about him that…oh, I don't know, and I'm just… (*With increasing frustration.*) Well, quite honestly I get tired of it. I get tired of feeling like that, of feeling that… corrupted. I'm *so* sick of being so suspicious of every bloody thing and everybody all the bloody time. I'm sick and tired of having to feel as though everyone's on the make, and nothing's what it seems, and everything's too good to be true, and being cynical and being bitter and jaundiced about every single bloody thing in this life! I'm sick of it! I am, really! And I just didn't want to be like that for once. I just didn't. I wanted to believe him, that's all.

(*Pause.*)

JACK: (*Putting his arm around her.*) Oh, Rachel. (*Beat.*) I don't know what to tell you. I mean, what you say is all very commendable, but…well, Christ, love, you're about two generations out of sync with the times. You've got your heart in the right place but you've got your head stuck up your arse. The fact is life's *not* nice. Nice if it was, but it's not. The fact is, it's vicious and it's two faced. It's all self-service these days. They've all got dirt under their fingernails, all of them. They're all grubbing around for one thing or another. Whatever you'd like it to be, the truth is you can't trust anyone and nothing *is* what seems. And unless you wise up to that, you're going to find yourself on the endangered species list – along with the pandas and the whales and the spotted toads.

RACHEL: How pretty you make it sound. How worthwhile. (*Beat.*) Anyway, I don't care. I don't care if what I did was foolhardy or naive. The experience I had today was something I'll never forget for the rest of my life. It felt…magical. I felt like a child again. And whatever *it* was, it made me want to believe again. In what, I don't know, but it did. I believed, and I'm so, *so* glad I did. It's changed me, Jack, it really has. I'm not the same person that left this house this morning. And it's a change for the better.

JACK: Well, that's some consolation. I'll let you know when I spot the difference.

(*Pause. RACHEL stares at Jack for some time.*)

RACHEL: Do you...Can you even recall what it was that made you want to marry me in the first place?

JACK: Of course I can – you were pregnant.

(*RACHEL looks away. JACK feigns an expression of innocence.*)

JACK: A little humour...trying not to be so cynical, as per your request.

RACHEL: And how naturally it comes to you.

JACK: Now who can't take a joke? I thought you were the one that wanted life on the light side? Anyway, it's bloody late and I've got to be at work tomorrow – and I assume you do too, unless you're planning on spending the day in the company of your crackpot codger again – so perhaps we could wrap this up before the chiming of the witching hour, if that's all right with you?

RACHEL: Wrap it up? (*She stares at him for a moment before sitting back down on the sofa.*) All right, I'll wrap it up. We arrived at his flat shortly thereafter – it was just around the corner, as it turned out, and–

JACK: That was convenient.

RACHEL: And not at all what I'd imagined. I think I half expected to see piles of tarot cards and beaded curtains. I even blurted out, in my nervousness, some lame quip about him flashing me his crystal balls. (*To herself.*) Christ, whatever was I thinking? (*Finishing her drink.*) He laughed and smiled, of course, but it was in a way that I could tell was more to save me from embarrassment than anything else, which, naturally, just increased my embarrassment. (*Beat.*) The odd part was, his home was the epitome of ordinary: nice, cozy…but completely and utterly unremarkable. Almost deliberately so…almost as if he'd planned it that way. I know that sounds daft, but… (*Beat.*) Anyway, so I sat on the sofa, he in an armchair. He asked if I'd like a cup of tea, which, of course, I hurriedly declined, having already consumed close to fifteen thousand cups that afternoon. And then he asked me, "How's Jack's mother?"

(*Pause.*)

JACK: (*Warily.*) And why did he ask that?

RACHEL: I didn't know. So I said, "She's fine."

JACK: Be very careful, Rachel.

RACHEL: Then he asked me if it had spread. I told him it hadn't; that they'd managed to remove everything before it had had the chance. I said that the doctors had agreed that her prognosis looked very good and she should be out of the hospital in a week or so.

JACK: (*With studied censure.*) How dare you.

RACHEL: What?

JACK: How dare you discuss my mother's illness with a complete stranger. How dare you bandy her cancer about like it was yesterday's leftover gossip!

RACHEL: But I didn't, Jack, *I didn't*. And what's more, I'd never even mentioned your name either. I'd spoken of you, of course, many times in the conversation, but never by name. I'd always referred to you as "my husband."

JACK: This isn't funny, Rachel, whatever *this* is. I don't know what you told him or what you're trying to prove, but it's not funny. There are some things you don't joke about – you just don't.

RACHEL: I know, and I didn't. But that's what he said. And then he asked me…

   (*Beat.*)

JACK: What?

RACHEL: (*With an awkward laugh.*) He asked me…what was the most humiliating thing that had ever happened to me.

JACK: And?

RACHEL: I said…God, it's so stupid now. It sounded stupid when I told him.

JACK: (*Impatiently.*) What?

RACHEL: I told him about the time when I was…oh, I don't know…twelve or thirteen, I suppose, in Mr. Evans history class. I explained to him that I'd only ever been an average pupil at best, and had always seen myself as something just shy of a thicko. Not that I was alone. There always seemed to be plenty of others in the class whose academic aptitude rivaled my own. The difference was they never seemed to care. They'd giggle or shrug or mouth obscenities under their breath about this person or that person – or more often than not Mr. Evans. The difference was I did care. I wanted to be clever. I didn't think I was, but it didn't stop me wanting to be. I wanted the teachers to think of me as special. I wanted the class to admire and applaud me, or sneer and hate me because I was so gifted and brilliant. I knew I wasn't and never would be. I knew I didn't have that...that capacity, I suppose. I was hopeless at remembering facts or figures or times and dates. I'd try, but I couldn't – it wasn't in me. But it never stopped me wanting to feel clever. (*Beat.*) Anyway, one day...one day Mr. Evans posed a question to the class in such a way, and with such grave misgiving in his voice, that you would have thought that the entire fate of civilization rested upon its answer, and that there wasn't one among us who could save us from our hideous fate. And yet, miraculously, for some inexplicable reason, I knew it! I knew the answer! I immediately thrust my hand into the air, reaching up as high as I could. I stretched my arm until it hurt, hoping, *hoping* with every sinew and muscle that he would notice mine from amongst the others, so that I could prove myself, and show him and everyone else that I wasn't stupid or dense, and that I really *did* care. (*Beat.*) Then, to my utter amazement, he raised his intimidating finger at pointed it directly at me. "Yes, Rachel?" he boomed. And I froze. (*Beat.*) I couldn't say it. I knew it, but I just couldn't say it. Nerves, I suppose, but I was petrified. I couldn't speak properly. I started mumbling and stuttering, and I...and before I could think straight or knew what was happening he'd let out this deep sigh and pointed to someone else, who, of course, knew the answer instantly and gave it without the slightest hesitation. (*Beat.*) I think it was his sigh that hurt the most: as if he never really believed I'd know the answer but thought he'd show everyone his largess by taking a risk on that stupid girl in the fifth row.

(*Beat.*)

JACK: And that was it?

RACHEL: Yes…that was it.

JACK: That was your most humiliating moment? I'd say you were lucky – I can think of a lot worse myself.

RACHEL: I wouldn't doubt it for a second. But at that moment – in the context of our conversation – that's what came to mind.

JACK: And what did this prove, exactly?

RACHEL: In and of itself – nothing, I suppose. But then…then he smiled and said, "Are you sure, Rachel?" And I said, "Yes." And then he reached into the inside pocket of his jacket and pulled out a scarf – a silk scarf.

JACK: Oh, how perfect – like a second-rate magician.

RACHEL: Yes, Jack, like a second-rate magician. And as he held the scarf between his fingers he said to me, "Are you sure *this* isn't the most humiliating experience you've ever had?" And, of course…he had me.

JACK: What's that supposed to mean?

RACHEL: It means I couldn't argue with him. It means he'd called my bluff.

JACK: By waving a scarf at you?

RACHEL: Yes. Well, no...not a scarf... (*Reaching into the inside pocket of her jacket.*) This scarf.

(*Pause.*)

JACK: Oh, he gave it to you, how sweet: a little memento.

RACHEL: Yes. And now I'm giving it to you. (*Holding it forth.*) Here, take it.

JACK: I don't want it – I don't want some old man's scarf.

RACHEL: It's hardly his, Jack; a bit too chi-chi for him I'd say, wouldn't you? He's just forwarding it. It's Melanie's.

(*Beat.*)

JACK: Melanie's?

RACHEL: Yes, Melanie's. It's hers and we think it ought to be returned to her.

JACK: Melanie's?

RACHEL: Yes, Jack, Melanie – you do remember Melanie, don't you? You work with her every day...to say the least. Surely her name must ring a bell or two?

JACK: What the hell makes you think it's Melanie's?

RACHEL: Oh, I don't know...the vivid colours? The pungent smell of a Chanel No. 5 knock-off? The fact that I found the tail end of it poking out from beneath our bed?

JACK: (*Aggressively.*) What is this?

RACHEL: It's a scarf.

JACK: It's a game.

RACHEL: (*Calmly.*) It's a scarf. (*Still proffering the scarf.*) Here, take it – it won't bite.

JACK: Don't give it to me, I don't want your creepy old man's voodoo props – God knows where it's been.

RACHEL: Don't be silly, Jack, you know exactly where it's been. It's Melanie's. I've seen her wearing it often. It's obviously a favourite. Which is why I'm sure she'd be very relieved to have it returned.

(*Pause.*)

JACK: All right, that's enough – knock it off.

RACHEL: Knock what off?

JACK: All this crap! All this glass-eyed freak crap. She put you up to this, did she?

RACHEL: Who?

JACK: I said knock it off didn't I? Melanie, who else? Pulled you aside, I suppose, and drilled you full of poisonous thoughts? This is your little game, is it, the two of you? This is your "Let's fuck with Jack?" (*Beat.*) Stupid tart, I knew she'd never have the balls

26

to keep her mouth shut. This was your idea, was it? Well of course it was, what am I saying? She'd be hard pressed to come up with two brain cells to rub together, let alone cobble together something this twisted. This is much more your style.

RACHEL: I still don't know what you're talking about.

JACK: There's no end to you is there? I know what you're like – all of you. Especially her. It's like they always say: If they can't keep their twat shut they can't keep their trap shut. She always said she'd do it. "It's her or me, Jack," "If you won't do it I will, Jack." (*Pause.*) Not that you care or I care but she really wasn't anything. Nothing at all. Just a cheap fuck. She came off as the type that wanted it bad enough that once they'd had it you'd think that would be it. But not her. A couple of drinks and a sit-down pizza and you'd think I'd proposed. Started getting pushy. I couldn't get rid of her. Started wanting more and more. Started making threats. I ignored it in the beginning. Who wouldn't – some brainless tart from Streatham going through the motions? Then she starts ringing here. Nothing to say...just wanted to "talk." That's when I knew. I knew it was just a matter of time. (*Beat.*) So you needn't bother looking so smug and pleased with yourself with your little Roald Dahl yarn – it was all half expected anyway.

RACHEL: And no remorse, Jack...not even now?

JACK: Remorse? You've got some nerve, you have. After I've sat up here half the night, not knowing if you were alive or dead. Not knowing where the hell you were as you waltz in here and start spinning me some mind-fuck about some old pervert and my mother's cancer? Why the hell would I be feeling anything that resembles remorse? Pity is more like it.

RACHEL: But it wasn't a yarn – I just told you what happened, that's all.

JACK: See, that's half your problem: you don't know when to stop. You never did. You never let anything go; you always have to stretch it out into some never ending soap opera. It was too much, Rachel. You're too much. You suffocate. I'm only human, for God's sake. I only did what anyone else would've done – I needed some breathing space, that's all. I needed an outlet.

RACHEL: For your plug?

JACK: Very good. (*Beat.*) For my head. And tonight's the best example of all. Any normal person would've walked in here and said, "Jack, I know you're having an affair with Melanie – what are we going to do about it?" But not you, you've got no time for logic or common sense. You have to spend hours stitching together some ludicrous cock and bullshit story whose sole purpose is to fuck with my head. Is it any wonder…I mean, really, is it? (*Beat.*) Did it make you feel better?

RACHEL: Did what make me feel any better, Jack? Having you wait up into the night, wondering all the time where I was? Having you worry and fret about who I was with or what I was doing? Having nasty, insidious thoughts clawing their way into your mind as you tried like a fool to pretend to yourself that everything was all right? No, it didn't. Not really. (*Pause.*) But perhaps…perhaps if everybody knew but you, because you were too cowardly or naïve to face the obvious; perhaps if you had your friends telling you that you were being made a mockery of; perhaps if you'd had the phone slammed down on you a dozen times the moment your voice was heard on the other end; perhaps if you'd smelled cheap perfume on your husband's jacket, on his shirts, on the sheets, in the car, up your nose, always, everywhere, lined to the inside of your nostrils like some noxious chemical you couldn't escape no matter where you went, no matter what you did, then yes, *yes*…I might have felt better.

(*JACK stares at RACHEL for a moment, before inhaling sharply through his nose.*)

JACK: Mmm…I never liked it either. After all these years it's a comfort to know we still have similar tastes. (*Rising and moving towards the door R.*) I'm going to bed. I'm tired, I'm pissed off, and I don't want to talk anymore. We can discuss options in the morning. And if you've an ounce of feeling or responsibility left in you, you'll call your mother – she'll be beside herself by now.

RACHEL: (*Looking back at him, as he reaches the door.*) Jack?

(*JACK stops and looks back at RACHEL.*)

RACHEL: Thanks for the worry, all the same.

JACK: (*After a moment, dispassionately.*) I'd have done the same for the cat.

(*JACK exits. After a moment RACHEL picks up the phone from the sofa and begins dialing.*)

RACHEL: It's me, did I wake you?…Good…Oh honestly, I can't right now; I'm sorry but I'm just so tired. I'll tell you tomorrow…No, it's fine, everything's fine…Yes, relatively speaking…Um…badly, I suppose, but I expected worse…No, not really. Listen, I…I want to thank you again…Well, for coming forward like that…I know, I know, but still…I think it was brave of you – very brave. I mean you weren't to know how I'd react, were you? (*With an ironic laugh.*) That's a funny way of putting it...No, not a word – thinks I'm completely batty...Oh, I don't care, he can think what he likes...I've no idea. I imagine he'll confront her with it, she'll deny it, he won't believe her and that'll be the end of it. (*After a sigh.*) Anyway, let's talk tomorrow... No really, I'm fine, I'm fine, I am, it's just...well, it's going to take some adjusting to isn't it, being one again, instead of two? It hasn't really sunk in, I don't think...No, no, I know that, but...well, I'll just have to face it head on, won't I – and hopefully come out the other side with a little more insight. That's the plan, at least. (*Beat.*) Strange really, but you think you see these things coming long before they hit you, and when they do everything seems to move in slow-motion; and yet before you know what's happened...it's all over...finished...in the blink of an eye.

(*BLACKOUT.*)

END OF PLAY

ABOUT THE AUTHOR

From the Royal Court Theatre in London to the Playhouse Theatre in Tasmania, the works of award-winning playwright Andrew Biss have been performed across the globe, spanning four continents. His plays have won awards on both coasts of the U.S., critical acclaim in the U.K., and quickly became a perennial sight on Off-Broadway and Off-Off Broadway stages.

In London his plays have been performed at The Royal Court Theatre, Theatre503, Riverside Studios, The Union Theatre, The White Bear Theatre, The Brockley Jack Studio Theatre, Fractured Lines Theatre & Film at COG ARTSpace, and Ghost Dog Productions at The Horse & Stables.

In New York his plays have been produced at Theatre Row Studios, The Samuel French Off-Off-Broadway Festival, The Kraine Theater, The Red Room Theater, Times Square Arts Center, Manhattan Theatre Source, Mind The Gap Theatre, 3Graces Theatre Company, Emerging Artists Theatre, Curan Repertory Company, Pulse Ensemble Theatre, American Globe Theatre, The American Theater of Actors, and Chashama Theatres, among others.

His plays and monologues are published in numerous anthologies from trade publishers Bedford/St. Martin's, Smith & Kraus, Inc., Pioneer Drama Service, and Applause Theatre & Cinema Books.

Andrew is a graduate of the University of the Arts London, and a member of the Dramatists Guild of America, Inc.

For more information please visit his website at: andrewbiss.com

The Most Interesting Man in the
Whole Wide World

1M/3F Approx. 90 minutes

Horatio Higgins recently lost his job. He also lost his parents, so he claims, though the precise cause of their demise remains something of an enigma. Living alone in his tiny flat, Horatio's sense of isolation is mitigated only by a near-continual dialogue with himself and by the companionship of what he affectionately describes as "my wife."

Things change, however, when he encounters a sweet, impressionable young woman named Nore. As their relationship lurches unsteadily forward, Horatio finds himself struggling against a riptide of conflicting realities that he is ill-equipped to cope with until events at last overtake him and a new yet oddly familiar reality emerges.

The End of the World

5M/3F Approx. 90 minutes

Valentine's parents have decided that the time has finally come for their son to leave home and discover life for himself. As he ventures forth into the vast world beyond, his new adventure is soon drawn to a halt when he is mugged at gunpoint. Frightened and exhausted, he seeks shelter at a bed and breakfast establishment named The End of the World, run by the dour Mrs. Anna. Here Valentine encounters a

Bosnian woman with a hole where her stomach used to be, an American entrepreneur with a scheme to implant televisions into people's foreheads, and a Catholic priest who attempts to lure him down inside a kitchen sink. Then things start getting strange...

In this story based loosely around the state of Bardo from The Tibetan Book of the Dead - an intermediate state where the dead arrive prior to rebirth - dying is the easy part. Getting out of Bardo and returning to the land of the living is a far more perilous proposition, and unless you know what you're doing...you might never leave.

An odd, yet oddly touching tale of life, death, and the space in-between.

Leah's Gals

3M/5F Approx. 90 minutes

Leah's just won the lottery in what she describes as "the biggest single, one-time cash haul in this here dirt-poor, shitty state's history!" But, rather than living the highlife, Leah decides to split the winnings among her three daughters, asking only for a deathbed-style declaration of love in return. When her youngest daughter, Patina, scoffs at the idea, Leah disowns her with vitriolic fury. Bestowing instead the prize money upon her two eldest daughters, her dreams of a pampered retirement in the arms of her offspring for herself and her close companion, Pearl, seem guaranteed. Things soon turn sour, however, as long-held grievances and newfound wealth lead to familial treachery, violence and death.

Greed, lust, drugs, and Capodimonte combust in this low-rent, Southern fried twist on a literary classic.

The Meta Plays

A collection of short comedic plays that take theatrical conventions on a metaphysical joyride.

This unique compilation of wittily inventive short comedies can be performed by as few as 4 actors or as many as 18, all with minimal set and prop requirements. Many of these plays have gone on to receive highly successful productions around the world, garnering glowing reviews along the way.

Arcane Acts of Urban Renewal

Five One-Act Comedies Approx. 100 minutes

A collection of five thematically related, darkly humorous one-act plays in which ordinary people find themselves in the most extraordinary circumstances.

An Honest Mistake: Madge has long since surrendered herself to the verbal abuse doled out to her by her belligerent husband, Stan. On this particular evening, however, her fears of a rat beneath the floorboards, combined with her absent-mindedness, result in her dishing up Stan not only his evening meal - but also his just deserts!

A Familiar Face: Two elderly women, old friends, meet up in a London café shortly after one them – Dora – has been widowed. As Dora's grief and anger intensifies, her good friend Eydie begins to suspect there may be more to her angst than the loss of a loved one. When Dora calmly removes from her shopping bag a large glass jar containing a human head, discussions over its mysterious identity, and how it came to be lodged in the cupboard under her stairs, lead to some startling revelations.

A Slip of the Tongue: Miss Perkins, tired of the constant innuendos and sexual insinuations of her employer, Mr. Reams, has decided to hand in her notice. On this particular morning, however, Mr. Reams decides to take things one step further. Unfortunately, due to Miss Perkins' nervous disposition and a telephone that rings at a disturbingly high pitch, he soon discovers he's bitten off more than he can chew...or at least, one of them has.

An Embarrassing Odour: Ethel, a widowed pensioner, sits down one evening to tackle her daily crossword puzzle. Suddenly her tranquil world is turned upside down when a burglar enters her home, believing it to be unoccupied. As Ethel vainly attempts to forge a relationship with the violent delinquent before her, his concerns lie only with getting his hands on her valuables...that and the unpleasant smell that fills the room. What is that smell?

A Stunning Confession: During an evening in front of the television a staid married couple suddenly find themselves having to confront a new reality.

A Ballyhoo in Blighty

The multi-award winning, critically acclaimed "Indigenous Peoples" (Winner "Best Play" – New York's Wonderland One-Act Festival) is paired with three other cheeky, uproarious comedies in what is guaranteed to be an unforgettable, side-splitting evening's entertainment.

Also included are "The Man Who Liked Dick", "Kitchen Sink Drama" and "Carbon-Based Life Form Similar" – all outrageously funny British comedies that have received lauded productions in London, New York and beyond.

Cast size: 4M / 5F (Roles can be doubled for a 2M/2F cast configuration)

15898189R00026

Printed in Great Britain
by Amazon